Kierkegaard and the Mermaid

For Marita Faden and Franck Babin
L. F.-B.

Kierkegaard
and the Mermaid

Narrated by
Line Faden-Babin and Jakob Rachmanski

Illustrated by
Lucia Calfapietra

Translated by
Jordan Lee Schnee

Plato & Co.
diaphanes

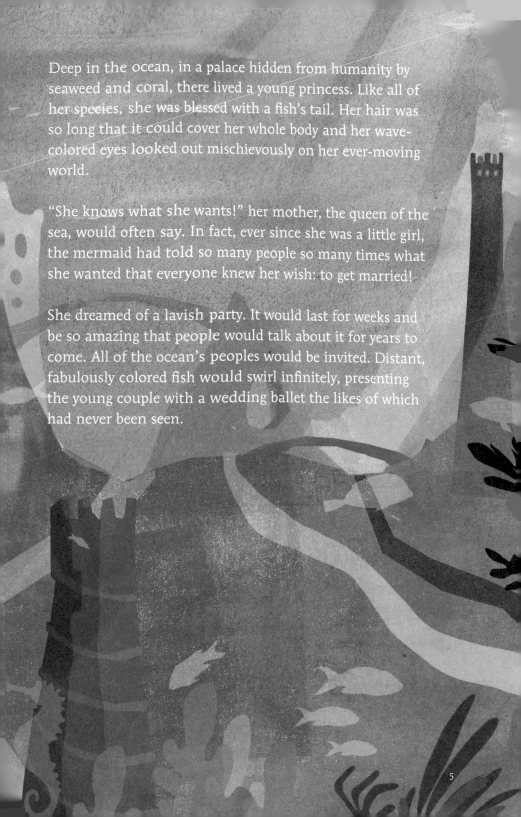

Deep in the ocean, in a palace hidden from humanity by seaweed and coral, there lived a young princess. Like all of her species, she was blessed with a fish's tail. Her hair was so long that it could cover her whole body and her wave-colored eyes looked out mischievously on her ever-moving world.

"She knows what she wants!" her mother, the queen of the sea, would often say. In fact, ever since she was a little girl, the mermaid had told so many people so many times what she wanted that everyone knew her wish: to get married!

She dreamed of a lavish party. It would last for weeks and be so amazing that people would talk about it for years to come. All of the ocean's peoples would be invited. Distant, fabulously colored fish would swirl infinitely, presenting the young couple with a wedding ballet the likes of which had never been seen.

5

One morning while the kingdom was still in slumber, a
shadow glided silently through the aquatic palace. Responding
to a minute ripple of turbid water, it made for the alcove
where the young mermaid was lying.

It was a little porbeagle shark with a silvery back and white
belly. It played at camouflaging itself in the multicolored
walls of anemones. Huge pieces of seaweed shuddered as
it passed. With one last thrust of its tailfin, the porbeagle
glided soundlessly through the half-light until it reached the
princess' bed.

But it was in for a shock—on the blue seaweed mattress it only
found a pile of shells! The princess was gone.

Then a tinkling laugh rang out through the room:
"*I* tricked you this time!"

As the luminescent jellyfish came out of hiding, bringing with
them a soft light, the porbeagle started to wag his tail and
hurried towards his owner, the young mermaid, doing a few
barrel rolls on the way.
"I don't have time for you today," announced the princess.
"I'm in a rush! I'm supposed to meet my future husband
tonight!"

It was true—the King and Queen of the Sea were hosting a ball
in their daughter's honor. They had invited the kingdom's most
prominent mermen so that her dream could become a reality.

As the guests entered the aquatic palace, they were amazed by the sumptuous decorations. The floor was paved with mother of pearl and finished with the kingdom's most beautiful pearls. The walls were adorned with precious coral and rare shells, and hung with shining mirrors. Lovely melodies echoed down off the columns. Getting closer, mermaids could be seen on top, playing harps and blowing into massive shells. The royal couple was seated at the very back of the hall, surrounded by representatives and prominent members of the large sea monsters. They were eagerly waiting for the show to start.

Finally, the princess appeared. The hubbub stopped, and an amazing thing happened—in the grotto, the water cleared, not a single bubble troubling it. The enraptured guests held their breath. Then the waves lost their glasslike quality, and a murmur of wonder escaped the crowd. It rang for a long time through the vaulted chambers.

The mermaid approached the center of the room. A first suitor asked her to dance. The princess found it difficult to spin gracefully in his arms and was disappointed. He was too small for her—far from who she had imagined as her future husband.

As soon as the music had stopped, a second merman invited her to dance. This one was too thin for her taste and always against the current. He was a horrible dancer.

The mermaid gave a dance to each of her suitors, one by one, without ever feeling completely satisfied, until there was just one left.

The last merman approached. He was the most beautiful of them all.

He led the mermaid into a waltz. His elegance charmed her. Catching her reflection in one of the hanging mirrors, she could not keep the smile from her lips. She had seen the mermaid she had always dreamed of being. She was sure of it. She had finally found the perfect merman, the one she wanted to marry. There was never a happier mermaid than our mermaid on that night.

The next morning, the mermaid could tell something was out of place before she even opened her eyes. She felt a painful anxiety, like one stormy day when she had swum against a powerful current that pushed her back unceasingly. She had exhausted herself and had not even moved closer to her destination. She opened then closed her eyes, trying to chase away her despair.

Lying rigid on her seaweed bed, the princess was about to start sobbing when her porbeagle shark, who knew her so well, came to comfort her, rubbing his muzzle against her shoulder. Its beloved mistress seemed lost:
"What's this anxious feeling? Why did it bubble up at the moment when I should be the happiest mermaid in the world?"
She kept thinking:
"Is it my merman? But he's the most beautiful of them all!"
For a few seconds, the mermaid relived her dancing with her fiancé. As she let the memories of the ball come back to her, she realized that she had barely concerned herself with the preparations. Her parents had chosen the venue and which suitors would be invited all by themselves. She remembered how much her mother and father had applauded when she had chosen her future husband. Suddenly, she was filled with doubt: "Was it actually me who chose my fiancé?"

In the grips of great turmoil, the princess left her room, her porbeagle on her heels. She had the appalling feeling that all of her choices had been made by other people. "But I want to be in charge of my life!" she fumed, picking up her pace.

The mermaid went past the chamber where her parents received the different peoples of the sea in the morning. Feeling feverish, she slipped inside.

The huge hall was deserted. No one was up yet after the previous night's ball. Only the king and queen were there, talking quietly. As she approached, the mermaid felt afraid of how they might react. After greeting them, she ventured: "Dad, Mom... Why... Why do I have to get married?"

Her parents stared for a moment, stunned.
They answered in unison:
"Because you have to!"
Her mother was smiling at her, but the mermaid was too overwhelmed to notice—everything seemed meaningless to her now.
"I have to? So, it's an illusion to think that I can even decide?" she asked.

The queen tried to console her. The king turned to the porbeagle, hoping it would help him understand his daughter's mood, but unfortunately the shark was racing a flounder at the other end of the hall, completely indifferent to the situation.

The princess had grown livid. Her voice trembled with anger: "Whatever I do, marriage or no, I am going to regret it because it won't be my decision! Whatever happens, I have no choice!"

That very day, the mermaid let it be known that she was breaking off the engagement. This angered her parents, hurt her suitor, and offended the peoples of the sea, but she didn't reconsider her decision.

She was in misery. Nobody understood her, and she felt the urge rise up within her to flee the life that was making her unhappy. On a whim, she made her decision: without knowing where she was off to, she left her undersea palace.

She swam, swam, and swam some more until she was out of the kingdom. She could picture her parents and her porbeagle worrying. How she wished things could be like they used to be, before she knew unhappiness!

Looking around, she saw she was lost. Way up above, a great light was causing the plankton to undulate in the waves. With an agile swish of her tail, the mermaid took refuge behind a shipwreck. Her heart beating fast, she sheltered in the shadow of the dark hull. All around her, the sea was calm and the fish kept going in their wild circles without seeming frightened. Realizing that there was no danger, the mermaid approached the astonishing light. Swimming towards it, she found herself directly under the quays of Copenhagen.

When she reached the surface she let out a cry of surprise and fear. She was dazzled.

It was a beautiful day. The sky was clear. The sun's rays played on the waves around the mermaid.

Blinking her eyes, she observed the hubbub on the wharf. Men were unloading boats, carrying huge cloth sacks on their backs. Fishmongers were hawking the catch of the day, haranguing housewives who, in white aprons, baskets in hand, would stop in front of a stall to examine, buy, or haggle for fish.

The smell of coffee and spices wafting out of a long ship was the first aroma to come tickle the mermaid's nose.

She forgot all about her sadness. The princess had never seen so many captivating objects and beings. Why had she always lived in the depths of the sea if the world was overflowing with such wonders?

Then the mermaid watched the strolling people. She was especially interested in the women who went by in the soft rustle of their dresses. They were so beautiful! What lightness, what graceful carriage! To walk on two legs, body stretched skyward!

"Oh, how I'd love to be a complete woman!"

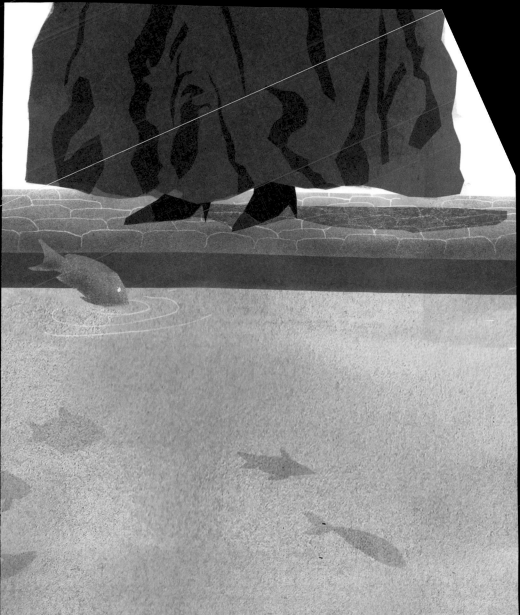

Shame seized her as she looked at her own body: she was naked and what was worse, cursed with a fish's tail! She noticed a piece of sail lying next to the quay and she wrapped herself in it, then sat down on the edge of the canal.

Once she was dressed, the mermaid started to notice the curiosity the passers-by were showing towards her. Despite her lowly dress, the men looked at her admiringly, while the women cast jealous glances at her golden hair.

Enjoying being the object of so much desire, the mermaid savored the Copenhagener's interest in her. After a while though, the fun flattened, giving way to a feeling of slight boredom.

She decided to cross to the other side of the canal, hoping to find a new distraction.

There she found more strollers, who observed her with similar interest. She could smell new aromas, and the atmosphere seemed slightly different. Yet nothing seemed as fantastic to her as when she had emerged from the sea a little while earlier.

And so the despair rose again within her. Gazing down, she saw her own reflection in the surface of the canal. She realized that, even with her fish tail hidden, she would never be like the beautiful ladies who came and went on the quays.

The mermaid felt her throat tighten. Her vision clouded, and she had to squint to keep seeing her reflection in the water. At that moment the silhouette of a man who had been walking came up beside her.

The mermaid looked up, and found herself face to face with a
fairly young man. He greeted her and smiled.

"Did you loose something in the water?" he asked.

"No, I'm just here, looking at reflections."

"And what do you see?" asked the man who had been strolling,
interested.

"I see a creature who is half woman, half fish. And now there is a
complete young man by my side."

"A complete man?" he said. "Yes, well anyway I am trying to become a complete man!"
"You're trying?" asked the mermaid, astonished. "Weren't you born human?"

The stroller let out a deep laugh and replied:
"Yes, I was born human. But we aren't born complete, we become it—it's about choice!"

The mermaid did not understand how you could choose to become a complete man, but before she could ask him a question, the man spoke again:
"What's so interesting to you about your reflection? Is something new going on?"

"Yes, I look miserable. But it's not usually like that! Just yesterday I was the most beautiful, happiest mermaid in the world," lamented the princess.

The man scratched his chin, looking pensive, then decided to introduce himself:
"My name is Søren Kierkegaard," he told her. "If you don't mind me saying, maybe you don't look different today… Maybe it's that how you see yourself is in the process of changing? Maybe this despair that you are discovering was always present?"

The mermaid frowned, but did not answer.

"Is it because of your problems that you are here?" Kierkegaard tried again.

"Yes," admitted the mermaid, blushing slightly. "I thought that my sadness had to do with my life in the kingdom at the bottom of the sea. And then, when I discovered your world, for a few hours I thought that I had finally found the place I could be happy in. Until today, I had never felt the sun's caress on my skin. Here I discovered smells that evoke far-off worlds, and the women's wonderful clothes ..."

"Well then! Are those sensations gone now?" asked Kierkegaard. "No, but they aren't a true cure. Just now my hopelessness returned completely. I think that deep down, I don't really resemble the princess that everyone sees me as. I'm afraid I don't exist. I'm not even sure if I want to get married! So what good are all this city's beautiful dresses and perfumes?" lamented the mermaid.

At its most basic, philosophy is about learning how to think about the world around us. It should come as no surprise, then, that children make excellent philosophers!

Plato & Co.'s clear approach and charming illustrations make this series the perfect addition to any little library.

Plato & Co.

DIAPHANES

The University of Chicago Press distributed by

Great
thinkers
viewed from
unusual angles.
Kirkus Reviews

Damn cool coffee
table books.
A. V. Club

NEWTON
AND THE
CLUB OF
ASTRONOMERS

PROFESSOR
KANT'S
INCREDIBLE
DAY

THE GHOST
OF
KARL MARX

MISTER DESCARTES
AND HIS
EVIL GENIUS

THE DEATH
OF
SOCRATES

WITTGENSTEIN'S
RHINOCEROS

DIOGENES
THE
DOG-MAN

LAO-TZU
OR
THE WAY
OF THE DRAGON

LEIBNIZ,
OR THE BEST OF
ALL POSSIBLE
WORLDS

HANNAH
ARENDT'S
LITTLE
THEATER

KIERKEGAARD
AND
THE MERMAID

MARTIN
HEIDEGGER'S
GROUCH

DR. FREUD,
FISH WHISPERER

Kierkegaard offered her his best smile, as if that was the greatest thing he had ever heard. The mermaid stared at him, taken aback.

"That's wonderful," exclaimed Kierkegaard. "Really, that's great!"

The mermaid was exasperated.

"I'm six fathoms deep in muck," she thought to herself, "and he's as pleased as can be!"

"You have recognized your sadness," said Kierkegaard. "So you're further than most to becoming a complete person!"

This surprised the princess. She listened closely.

"To overcome your sadness, you should stop trying to be someone you're not—you need to choose yourself exactly as you are."
"But maybe I don't want to be myself," replied the mermaid in a quiet voice. "I don't want to be sad anymore, or keep on being a princess who doesn't know what she wants."

Kierkegaard replied:
"You can't choose to be someone besides yourself, but you are free to chose the way in which you will lead your life! Once you have chosen to fully be yourself, then you will no longer feel hopeless."

Raising an arm towards the horizon, Kierkegaard added:
"In choosing yourself, you will become what you have not yet dared to take responsibility to be. A complete mermaid. Free! You won't marry unless you really want to. You won't do it because that's what is done, or because your parents decided instead of you. And that's how it will be for all the choices you make. You alone will choose!"

Kierkegaard doffed his hat to say goodbye, then turned on his heels and melted into the chaos that reigned on the wharves. The mermaid watched him go until he had disappeared.

For a long while she didn't move, thinking about the strange conversation. Her gaze fell upon the piece of sail that was lying next to her. She threw it into the canal and exclaimed:
"I don't want to hide my fish tail anymore. From this day on, I'll chose myself exactly as I am!"

Then, for the first time since the ball, the mermaid felt like seeing the merman again. The one she had rejected. She wanted to get to know him. With a graceful flick of her tail, she dove into the water, and began to swim towards the kingdom under the sea, back to him.

In the days following their reunion, the mermaid observed that her fiancé was not only handsome but also funny and attentive. She also realized that he had certain flaws. He wasn't very talkative and had a horrible fear of moray eels. Above all, he was really bad at her favorite game: the lying fish. And he was a sore loser! The mermaid could clearly see that he didn't measure up to her image of him. And yet her love for him only deepened. She decided to choose the merman exactly as he was, and made it known that she wanted to marry him. The news filled him with joy, and the king and queen were relieved. The peoples of the sea approved.

The two fiancés decided to get married in private, far from the shining palaces of the undersea city. They chose a huge underwater reef that was known since ancient times and sculpted by the waves.

It was a magical place where the currents met. In the rock they had carved huge caves with polished arches. The stone was covered in white coral teeming with tiny silver fish.

When the ceremony was over, the newlyweds indulged in the pleasure of the tidal dance. The mermaid felt like they were now a single being, and she was filled with an incredible joy. They whiled away the day like that, in perfect harmony.

The mermaid had never felt so splendid. Even if day-to-day life was not only games and wonders, she did not want to spend a moment apart from her merman. She wanted to share everything with him, from the good times to the bad.

Now she saw things differently. Now she did not care about getting attention from others when she went for a swim, or having the last word in a conversation, for she, was at peace with herself. Her parents praised these changes in her again and again. The mermaid was pretty proud of herself too. From her point of view, she owed the transformation to herself alone.

One morning as she went passed a mirror, the young woman saw that her belly looked round. At first she was puzzled, but then she realized she was expecting a baby!

The princess collapsed onto the sand. Thinking it was a game, the porbeagle, who was never far, imitated her with a thud. But the princess was not playing games. She thought she would feel overjoyed, but now she only felt dark despair rising in her. She sat up, dizzy, having to lean against a stand of coral.

Since her marriage, the mermaid had managed to find answers within herself, but at that moment she realized she couldn't solve everything alone. She was not strong enough on her own.

When he found out he was going to be a father, the merman rejoiced. He did three flips and kissed the porbeagle, without realizing that it did not share in his wave of enthusiasm. When the mermaid confided in him that she was feeling anguished, he tried to reassure her as best he could, but she hardly felt understood. She sighed and sobbed—why couldn't she be happy?

In the palace's great hall, the princess' parents tried to comfort her.

"Why are you always making waves when things are simple?" the king finally asked her.

"How can you be sad when the most beautiful moment of your life just happened?" asked the queen.

Their words echoed through the vault like accusations. The mermaid hung her head.

"Get a hold of yourself. You need to believe in yourself!" her mother exclaimed. Her father agreed.

"But that's exactly what I can't do!" sobbed the mermaid.

In the days that followed, the mermaid felt sadder than ever. She could no longer stand her husband or parent's company. Even the porbeagle shark, which had finally learned to fetch the fish bones thrown for it, could not get a smile out of her. The more her family urged her to forget her troubles, the more she felt like she had to leave. One morning she could not take it anymore. She fled the undersea palace and swam to Copenhagen.

When the mermaid reached the quays, it was getting dark.
The last lamplighters were leaving with heavy steps. Everyone was gone. The only sounds were an accordion and the waves lapping at the hulls of boats. Soon the music stopped.

The mermaid felt like the wharves were different at night.
The shadows cast on the buildings' walls looked alive. The boats creaked strangely. Suddenly, the mermaid flinched. A sailor was shouting at her, a bottle in his hand. Frightened, she dove into the water, then swam aimlessly through Copenhagen's canals for a long time.

When dawn finally came, the mermaid was awoken by the cries of fishermen emptying their barrels of herring. The wharves filled up with merchants, housewives, and people out for a stroll.

After a while, the mermaid was happy to hear a familiar voice. She hoisted her head up over the edge of the quay, and saw Kierkegaard deep in conversation with an old merchant. The mermaid quickly got onto the wall that ran along the canal and tried to attract her friend's attention. He finally saw her and hurried over, asking how she was doing.

"Horrible!" answered the mermaid. "I found out that I'm pregnant, and I guess I'm supposed to be happy, but really it feels like the world is falling apart. My feeling of misery came back! And I don't even know why!" she lamented, wiping her eyes.

Sitting down beside her, Kierkegaard offered her his handkerchief. The mermaid pushed it away brusquely, her sadness giving way to anger.
"It's all your fault! You told me if I became myself, my sadness would disappear! I followed your advice and look at how things ended up!" she exclaimed, gesturing at her stomach. "You lied to me—I still feel hopeless, and now I'm going to have a baby!"

Kierkegaard watched her crying for a short while, then sighed. Through her tears, the mermaid could see his deeply wrinkled forehead.

In a thin, pained voice, Kierkegaard murmured:
"I spoke the truth the first time we met. Our hopelessness is the proof that we haven't managed to truly be ourselves..."
"*Our* hopelessness?" repeated the mermaid in surprise.
"My mermaid friend, if only you knew how well I understand you! I too have yet to become a 'complete man,' as you so beautifully put it. The despair that lurks deep within you... I know it well."

Kierkegaard did not go on, looking off to contemplate the waves behind them.
"What to do?" whispered the mermaid.

After a long silence, Kierkegaard spoke again:

"In away it doesn't depend on us. To become ourselves, we would need someone else to provide us with the true measure of what we are."

"And who could do that?" asked the mermaid. She remembered how incapable her parents and husband had been to help her find a way out of her sadness.

"The one who created us," responded Kierkegaard. "The one who wanted you as you truly are. The one who I truly am. Hopelessness reminds us that we can't be ourselves without having God as a measure."

"You're trying to say that you have to believe in God to truly become yourself?"

Kierkegaard again let out a long sigh, and affirmed in a breath:

"If I dare!"

The mermaid was speechless. What was Kierkegaard afraid of?

"But why is it so difficult?" she asked. "If God is the being on which we can rely to stop our hopelessness, then it's not crazy to believe in him..."

Kierkegaard smiled at her sadly:
"There is nothing that objectively proves the existence of God," he said. "I can't see God with my senses, nor with my mind, so I can't be sure God exists. To abandon myself to God, then, would require extraordinary courage... It's like if I wanted to leap over these sixty-thousand leagues of water," he said, gesturing to the far-off sea. "I can only forbid myself from taking such a leap. Reason tells me that I would never be able to reach the other shore, and nothing proves that God would help me."

He approached the canal, the ends of his feet extending over the edge, into the void. Kierkegaard opened his arms, like he were about to jump, but did nothing.

He lowered his arms and sat down heavily next to the mermaid. She sat thoughtfully for a moment, then put her head on his shoulder. They stayed like that, as the day warmed.

A seagull's cry woke the mermaid. The sun was now at its peak. Straightening, she studied the spot that Kierkegaard had been sitting before she fell asleep. He was gone. There was only the sound of canal water lapping below her.

While her bewilderment wore off, the mermaid waited on the quay for Kierkegaard, but nobody appeared. As the afternoon wore on, church bells began to ring. The mermaid gave up. She took a deep breath, closed her eyes, and dove into the brine. Tasting its delicious freshness, she felt as if she were being washed of all the hopelessness that had gripped her. She felt herself being reborn.

Splashing through the canal, the mermaid felt light, free. At that moment, she felt her child move in her stomach for the first time.

Laughing with delight, she imagined Kierkegaard flying above the sea, abandoned to God's hands.

Trustingly, she let herself be borne to the sea floor. As she approached her kingdom, she marveled at its transparent waves and the little spirals of sand that the currents kicked up. She saw mermen building houses out of boulders, the women covering the roofs in seashells. Nearby, the porbeagle was playing hide-and-seek in a patch of seaweed.

When her husband welcomed her, he was radiating joy. She took his hands, placed them on her stomach and felt an immense love suffusing her whole body. This love brought her beyond her husband and child, towards the other mermen and mermaids, and to all beings who she had once disregarded. At that very moment, the mermaid had the feeling of being complete, of fully existing.

On Copenhagen's quays, life continued on its way, as if nothing had happened.

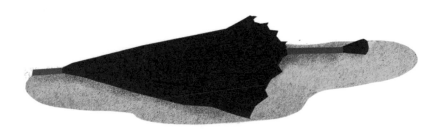

French edition:

Kierkegaard et la sirène

Line Faden-Babin, Jakob Rachmanski & Lucia Calfapietra

Design: Yohanna Nguyen et Avril de Perthuis

© Les petits Platons, Paris 2014

First edition

ISBN 978-3-0358-0141-5

© DIAPHANES, Zurich 2019

www.diaphanes.com

Layout: 2edit, Zurich

Printed and bound in Germany